World Art

Sue Nicholson

QEB Publishing

Written by Sue Nicholson
Designed by Susi Martin
Photographer Michael Wicks
Editor Paul Manning

Publisher Steve Evans
Creative Director Louise Morley
Editorial Manager Jean Coppendale

Printed and bound in China

The author and publisher would like to thank Millie
and Emily
Sarah Morley for making the models.

Picture credits
CORBIS/Caroline Penn 6, /Kevin Fleming 19, /Richard
Cummings 22
Getty Images/Steve Bly/Stone 15, /Bridgeman Art Library 17
The Art Archive/Musée des Arts Africains et Océaniens/
Dagli Orti 13
Travelsite/Neil Setchfield 9, 11
Werner Forman/British Museum 21

Note to teachers and parents/carers

The projects in this book are aimed at children in
grades 1 to 3 and are presented in order of difficulty,
from easy to more challenging. Each can be used as
a separate activity or as part of another area of study.
For example, the Native American war bonnet could
be linked to learning about Native American history.

While the ideas here are offered as inspiration,
children should always be encouraged to draw from
their own imagination and first-hand observations.

All projects in this book require adult supervision.

Sourcing ideas

★ Encourage the children to source ideas from their
   own experiences, as well as from books,
   magazines, the Internet, art galleries, or museums.
★ Ask them to talk about different types of art they
   have seen at home, on vacation, or on field trips.

★ Use the "Click for Art!" boxes as a starting point
   for finding useful material on the Internet.*
★ Suggest that each child keep a sketchbook
   of his or her ideas.

Evaluating work

★ Encourage the children to share and compare their
   work with others. What do they like best/least
   about it? If they did the project again, what would
   they do differently?
★ Help the children judge the originality of their work
   and to appreciate the different qualities in others'
   work. This will help them value ways of working
   that are different from their own.
★ Encourage the children by displaying their work.

* Website information is correct at the time of going to
  press. However, the publishers cannot accept liability
  for information or links found on third-party websites.

Contents

Words in bold, **like this**, are explained in the Glossary on page 24.

Getting started

This book will show you how to make amazing crafts from around the world. Here are some of the things you will need to get started:

Top tip

Don't forget to spread out some newspaper to work on, and wear an apron or an old shirt to keep your clothes clean

Basic equipment

- Sketchpad, pencils, and ruler
- Poster or **acrylic** paints
- Felt-tip pens
- Safety scissors
- White glue
- Hole punch

Any extra items are listed with each project.

Paper

Start a collection of:

- White posterboard or cardstock
- Colored paper
- Tissue paper
- Cardboard
- Silver foil

Craft foam

You can buy big sheets of colored craft foam. Some craft stores sell bags of precut foam squares and shapes

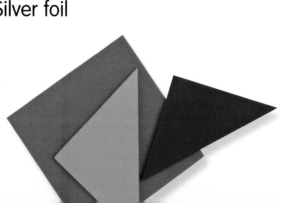

Craft supplies

Keep a big box full of things to decorate your crafts, for example:

★ Beads and buttons
★ Sequins and glitter
★ Scraps of tissue paper
★ Pieces of fabric, such as lace
★ Feathers, string, twine, and yarn

Salt and acrylic paints.

Glue

White craft glue is good for making things, but be careful not to get it in your eyes.

Paints and brushes

You will need:

● White **latex** paint
● Poster or acrylic paints
● A small brush for glue
● A medium-size paintbrush
● A small, thin paintbrush

Be careful!

Some projects involve cutting. Always ask an adult for help where you see this sign: ⚠

African cloth picture

In Benin, Africa, people tell stories in brightly colored cloth pictures. You can make your own picture using **felt**.

AGADJA 1708-1732

TEGBESSOU 1732-1774

KPENGLA 1774-1789

GUEZO 1818 1858

GLELE 1858-1889

BEHANZIN 1889-1894

A long time ago, cloth pictures like these hung behind the throne of the king of Benin.

Ask an adult to help you enlarge these animal shapes on a photocopier.

You will need:
- Felt (black, red, yellow, orange)

1 Draw an animal with felt-tip pen on the back of a piece of felt. Ask an adult to help you cut it out with scissors.

6

Top tip
Cut scraps of different-colored felt and glue them onto your animal shape.

Ask an adult to help you cut out a piece of black felt for your background. Make it at least 2 in (5 cm) bigger than your felt shape.

Cut out four strips of colored felt 1 in (3 cm) wide to make a frame. Overlap the strips at each corner and glue them in place.

4 Glue your animal picture in the middle of the black background.

Carnival mask

Make yourself a colorful decorated mask like the ones worn at **carnival** in Venice, Italy!

You will need:
- Cardboard
- Sequins, beads, and glitter
- Ribbon or elastic

1 Photocopy the mask shape below. Ask an adult to help you cut out the shape, then draw around it onto cardboard.

2 Ask an adult to help you cut out the cardboard mask shape.

3 Make holes in the sides of the mask with a hole punch.

4 Paint the mask in bright colors. When it is dry, glue on sequins or beads. You can also paint glue in a pattern, then sprinkle silver or colored glitter over it.

This person is wearing a traditional Venetian carnival mask.

Thread ribbon or
lastic through the
oles at the sides and
e the mask around
our head.

Click for Art!

To read about Venetian masks and costumes, go to:
http://english.comune.venezia.it/turismo/feste/carnevale/en_maschere.asp

Arabian mosaic

In **Islamic** countries such as Saudi Arabia, colored tiles are arranged in **geometric** shapes to make beautiful **mosaic** patterns.

1 Ask an adult to help you cut foam squares into triangles, then cut some of the triangles into smaller triangles.

2 Glue a square into the middle of a piece of white cardstock. Glue four small triangles around it.

You will need:
- Craft foam, cut into small squares
- White cardstock

3 Add four large triangle shapes …

4 … then eight small triangle shapes.

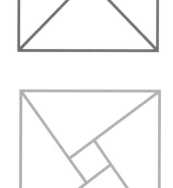

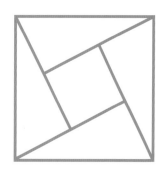

Try copying the shapes on the left to make exciting patterns of your own!

Click for Art!

To see an example of Islamic mosaic art, go to **www.metmuseum.org** and search on "Mihrab."

lamic tiles with hapes arranged a geometric attern.

6 Finish with eight arge triangles to orm a square.

Aboriginal painting

This project shows you how to paint a dot picture in the style of the Australian **Aboriginal** people.

1 Paint the whole paper pale yellow or orange. Leave to dry.

You will need:
- Acrylic or poster paints in rich, warm colors
- Cotton swabs

2 Ask an adult to help you copy the lizard shape below onto your picture. Paint it a rich, rusty red. Add wavy lines around it in dark orange or red and allow to dry.

3 Dip a cotton swab in white or yellow paint. Print rows of dots on the lizard's back and on some of the wavy lines.

Click for Art!

For examples of Aboriginal dot paintings, go to **www.thebritishmuseum.ac.uk/compass/** and search on "Aboriginal art."

12

Paint large orange
r red circles around the
zard. When the paint is
ry, print black or brown
nd white or red dots on
e circles.

Lively dot patterns and warm,
earthy colors are typical of
Aboriginal art.

Top tip

Arrange blobs of different-
colored paint in saucers.
Use a different cotton swab
for each color.

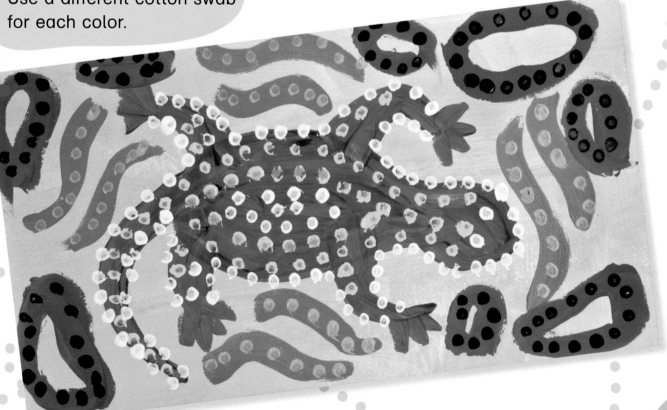

Native American war bonnet

Here's how to make a **Native American** headdress using feathers, string, and beads.

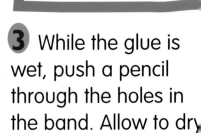

1 Ask an adult to help you cut a piece of cardboard 3 in (8 cm) wide and 4½–6 in (12–15 cm) long. Punch two holes in each side of the band.

2 Tear newspaper into strips 1 in (3 cm) wide and 2 in (6 cm) long. Glue three layers of strips to the band to make it thicker.

3 While the glue is wet, push a pencil through the holes in the band. Allow to dry.

4 Paint the band with white latex paint. When dry, paint patterns and pictures on the band.

You will need:
- Cardboard
- Newspaper
- White latex paint
- Feathers, string, and colored beads

Click for Art!

To see a traditional Arapaho headdress, go to **www.nativeamericans.com/Arapaho.htm**

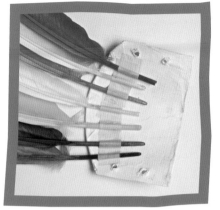

5 Glue or tape feathers behind the band so that they stick up from the top.

6 Tie strings through the bottom holes of the band so you can wear it around your head. Thread beads onto the strings and knot the ends so they don't slide off.

A Native American today wearing a traditional headdress.

Celtic brooch

Make yourself a brooch in the style of the ancient **Celts**.

You will need:

- Cardboard
- A small cup
- Foil
- Tracing paper
- Black poster paint
- Cotton balls
- A safety pin
- Masking tape

1 Draw around the rim of a cup onto cardboard. Ask an adult to help you cut out the circle.

2 Cut out a square of foil, 1½–2 in (4–5 cm) larger than the circle. Place the square over the circle and fold under the edges.

3 Choose a design and carefully trace over it with a soft pencil. Make the lines thick so the design stands out.

4 Place the tracing paper on the foil. Press hard over the lines with a pencil so you make marks in the foil.

Top tip
You can also paint your design on the circle with white glue and paint the brooch when the glue is dry. The gold brooch in the picture below has been made like this.

5 Rub black poster paint over the foil, then gently wipe it away with clean cotton balls so black paint is left in the grooves.

6 Tape a safety pin on the back of your brooch with masking tape, so you can wear it. You may like to glue a gemstone in the middle of your brooch.

Jewelry like this beautiful Celtic brooch is still made in Scotland and Ireland.

Click for Art!

For examples of Celtic brooches and bracelets, go to **www.thebritishmuseum.ac.uk/compass** and search on "Celtic jewelry."

Chinese paper dragon

At New Year, Chinese people dance in the street with huge paper and cloth dragons. Here's how to make a puppet dragon.

You will need:
- Colored cardstock or posterboard
- Sequins, glitter, and a "googly" eye
- Pair of chopsticks or Popsicle sticks

1 Trace the dragon's head and tail onto tracing paper, then onto cardboard. Ask an adult to help you cut out the shapes.

2 Paint both sides of a sheet of white paper bright red. When dry, fold the paper in half lengthwise and cut along the fold.

3 Fold the pieces of paper to form an **accordion**. Glue the two pieces of paper together to make one long piece for the dragon's body.

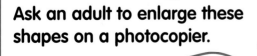

Ask an adult to enlarge these shapes on a photocopier.

Click for Art!

To learn about dragons in Ancient China go to **www.chinapage.com/dragon1.html**

The dragon dance is performed at Chinese New Year to bring good luck.

plastic "googly" eye

4 Paint the dragon's head and tail bright colors and glue on sequins, glitter, and "googly" eye.

5 Glue the head and tail to the dragon's body with white craft glue.

6 Glue the chopsticks or Popsicle sticks to the head and tail of the dragon.

Indonesian batik

Traditional **batik** uses hot wax and **dye** to make beautifully patterned fabrics. Here's a simple way to make a colorful batik flag.

You will need:

- Plain cotton cloth, such as muslin
- Pinking shears
- A white wax crayon
- A small paintbrush
- Cold-water dye, fixative, and salt
- Plastic bucket and rubber gloves

1 Ask an adult to help you cut the cloth into a rectangle 10 x 16 in (25 x 40 cm). Use pinking shears so the edge doesn't fray.

2 Draw a picture on one side of the cloth with a soft pencil.

3 Go over your design with the white wax crayon. (The dye will only color the part that have NOT been covered with wax.)

Click for Art!

To find out about Indonesian batik, go to:
http://members.tripod.com/aberges/

Using cold-water dye*

Wearing rubber gloves, wet the cloth in clean water. Pour dye into water in an old plastic bucket or bowl. Add salt and fixative according to the instructions. Stir well. Put the damp, unfolded cloth into the dye. Leave for one hour, stirring every 5 to 10 minutes. Rinse well in cold water.

*These instructions apply to Dylon® cold-water dye and fixative. For other brands, be sure to follow the manufacturer's instructions.

Batik cloth is made in Indonesia, in Southeast Asia.

Ask an adult to help
ou dye the cloth (see
e blue box, above).

When the cloth is
ry, glue a dowel stick
own one side on the
ack to make a flag.

21

Mexican Metapec sun

Mexican craftspeople make beautiful clay pottery. Here's how to make a **Metapec** clay sun to hang on your wall.

You will need:

- Air-drying clay
- A rolling pin
- A mixing bowl
- A blunt kitchen knife
- Bright acrylic or poster paints
- Paintbrushes
- String or twine

A typical Metapec clay sun from Mexico.

1 Soften the clay in your hands, then flatten it with a rolling pin. It needs to be about ½ in (1.5 cm) thick and a bit bigger than your mixing bowl.

2 Place a mixing bowl over the clay. Ask an adult to help you cut around the bowl with a dull knife.

3 Make holes for the eyes and mouth. Make clay eyes and eyebrows, a nose and mouth, and stick them on with a little water.

22

Top tip

To make your sun look happy or surprised, make faces in the mirror and copy how your mouth and eyes change.

4 Make clay rays to go around your sun's face. Press them firmly into place or stick them on with a little water.

5 Push a pencil through the top of the sun to make a hole for the string.

6 Let your sun harden, then paint it in bright colors. Thread string through the hole at the top so you can hang it on the wall.

Top tip

To make your clay sun look shiny, paint it with white glue mixed with water. The glue looks white when wet, but will be clear and shiny when it is dry.

Glossary

Aboriginal earliest people to live in Australia

accordion shape like an accordion or fan

acrylic easy-to-mix paint that can be cleaned with soap and water

batik way of decorating cloth using wax and colored dye

carnival happy festival, usually with a parade, music, and sideshows

Celts early tribal people of western Europe

dye powder or liquid used to color something, such as cloth

felt thick fuzzy cloth

geometric pattern made up of simple regular shapes, such as squares or triangles

Islamic from Islam, one of the world's main religions

latex paint type of water-based paint often used in painting walls

Metapec name given to a traditional Mexican clay sun

mosaic picture or pattern made up of lots of small squares of color

Native American earliest people to live in North America

Index